Thrift

The Ultimate 2 in 1 Box Set Guide to Making Money With Thrift Stores and Garage Sales in 60 Minutes or Less

Book # 1

Thrift Store

How to Earn $3000+ Every Month Selling Easy to Find Items From Thrift Stores, Garage Sales, and Flea Markets

Copyright © 2015

All rights reserved. No part of this book may be reproduced in any form without permission in writing from the author. Reviewers may quote brief passages in reviews.

Disclaimer

No part of this publication may be reproduced or transmitted in any form or by any means, mechanical or electronic, including photocopying or recording, or by any information storage and retrieval system, or transmitted by email without permission in writing from the publisher.

While all attempts and efforts have been made to verify the information held within this publication, neither the author nor the publisher assumes any responsibility for errors, omissions, or opposing interpretations of the content herein.

This book is for entertainment purposes only. The views expressed are those of the author alone, and should not be taken as expert instruction or commands. The reader of this book is responsible for his or her own actions when it comes to reading the book.

Adherence to all applicable laws and regulations, including international, federal, state, and local governing professional licensing, business practices, advertising, and all other aspects of doing business in the US, Canada, or any other jurisdiction is the sole responsibility of the purchaser or reader.

Neither the author nor the publisher assumes any responsibility or liability whatsoever on the behalf of the purchaser or reader of these materials.

Any received slight of any individual or organization is purely unintentional.

Table of Contents

Introduction

Chapter 1 - Financial Independence

Chapter 2- Thrift Stores, Garage Sales, and Flea Markets. Oh my!

Chapter 3- Discovering Your Niche

Chapter 4- Consumer Hunting

Chapter 5- Effectively Describing Items

Chapter 6 - Growing Profits to a Steady Income

Conclusion

Introduction

I want to thank you and congratulate you for downloading the book, "Thrift Store - How to Earn $3,000+ Every Month Selling Easy to Find Items From Thrift Stores, Garage Sales, and Flea Markets".

This book contains proven steps and strategies for earning $3,000+ every month selling easy to find items.

If you take the time to read this book fully and apply the information held within this book will help you to achieve financial freedom!

Thanks again for downloading this book, I hope you enjoy it!

Chapter 1: Financial Independence

So you want to become financially independent? Are you sick and tired of waking up in the morning, commuting through traffic, dealing with that horrible boss, and making other people filthy rich? People live most of their lives rushing to the punch-in clock day in and day out without any end in sight. It's no secret that not all of these people are happy with their lives. There is a much easier way to make a living in this slow economy and achieve pure financial freedom.

What if I told you there is a proven way for you to achieve complete financial freedom and live a truly happy and peaceful life? You could say goodbye to your dead-end job, work your own hours, be your own boss, and spend your time the way you want to spend it. Would you be interested in knowing this secret? Of course you would be, that is why you bought this book.

As with any proven method, it will take time, determination and effort to achieve absolute financial independence. Nothing in this world comes easy, so you will have to work to find the methods that best suit your situation. You are already off to a great start.

First of all, you must be and remain motivated. Take out a sheet of paper and write a brief paragraph on why you need to change your financial situation. Write another brief paragraph on the financial goals you expect to achieve. As you go through this book, write down how you are going to do it. Each day, take a look at this piece of paper until you have achieved your goal. Then burn or shred that piece of paper because you will no longer have to look back.

You may not have much money to start out with and that is absolutely fine. You may feel like a small fish in a big pond at first. That is the amazing part about starting out a venture such as this one. As long as youexactly follow exactly what we say here, by the time you reach chapter 6: Compounding Profits for a Steady Income, you will possess the information to turn yourself into a much bigger fish.

We will explore methods that will help you find and sell ordinary items at thrift stores, garage sales, and flea markets. All the information is literally at your fingertips. Remember that the moretime and effort you put into these working methods the more successful you will be.

Chapter 2: Thrift Stores, Garage Sales, and Flea Markets. Oh My!

The key to any successful financial endeavor is to find a need and fill it. In this chapter we will explore the many places you can find many goods that people will need. The amount capital you start with will determine how fast you will achieve your goal. You may start right now with almost nothing and build up your own business buying and selling secondhand goods.

We are a society of consumers that rely on supply and demand. The more in demand a product may be in your area, the easier it will be to sell. The smaller the supply of a product that is in demand, the more profit you can make. You have to be in the right place at the right time to find valuable stock to sell to your consumers.

We will speak more about consumers in Chapter 4: Consumer Hunting. For now, we need to focus on your stock; the product you will be marketing and selling.

Thrift Stores, Garage Sales, and Flea Markets are packed with secondhand "junk" that people no longer need or want. Even though they may have bought these products brand new at quadruple the price, they have depreciated in value. People are willing to part with these products that they, at one time, adored and are now willing to accept a very small amount of money from someone who will want them. Let's explore each one of these types of places where you can find secondhand goods.

1. Thrift Stores:

Thrift Stores can be found almost anywhere. You may already be familiar with the ones in or around your area. They are places that receive unwanted goods from people. Typically, they use the proceeds from the sales of these items for a charitable cause. This is where you will find anything from normal household objects to old overlooked vintage antique items that could be highly sought after.

Since these places rely mostly on donations, they have an almost unlimited stock of various items from the people in that area. Sometimes when people pass away they or their families may donate part or all of their belongings to a thrift store. This can be a hotspot for overlooked valuables.

How to find a good thrift store:

Using this method, you will find a thrift store that will have the most valuable goods at the prices you are willing to pay.

Begin with searching on whichever search engine you prefer. My preference is http://www.google.com so I will use that one as an example. Most if not all search engines have a local directory these days, so feel free to use your own.

Simply type in "Thrift Store" and click "Search". On Google, you will receive millions of results. Since we will want to look locally we will go to the top menu and click on "maps". You may have to put in your zip code to see results in your area.

Your results will be narrowed down to a much smaller number of thrift stores in your area. Navigate around the map or search through the listings in the areas you are looking in.

To determine which thrift stores you should be looking for, you should have a good idea on what type of capital you are working with. Try not to be intimidated by the word capital. It is just a fancy way of saying money; it is the amount of money you have available for use. In this case, the amount of money you have available to buy goods for resale.

You have no capital:

If you are starting out with little or no capital, there's still a way for you to start making money! Some thrift stores will take your unwanted items and give you a credit towards a purchase in their store. You should call around and ask which ones will do this. They don't care what types of items as long as they are sellable. It's time for you to go through the attic and garage. If you haven't seen it for over a year, you should part with it. You may be killing two birds with one stone because you'll probably need the storage for the items you are going to buy and sell.

You have low capital:

Look for thrift stores in low-income areas. These stores will be marketed towards lower income families. There, you will be able to find lower quality goods from donations given by lower-income families. Items here are sold at very low prices.

You have slightly higher capital:

Look for thrift stores in middle class-income areas. These stores will be marketed towards families with slightly higher incomes. There, you will be able to find moderate quality goods from donations given by middleclass families. Items here are sold at slightly higher prices.

You have very high capital:

Look for thrift stores in or around high class properties and high income residents. You will know the type of area in which to look by its appearance; they have gates at the front of their driveways, a lot of property, and help (maids, butlers, gardeners).

These stores will be marketed towards families on the middle class and higher-income fence. There, you will be able to find every kind of good including a lot of high quality goods at a fraction of the price.

Remember: When looking for products in thrift stores take the time to look through the whole store before picking any items for purchase to avoid impulse buying. No matter how great the item is, remember to keep your own impulses out of the equation. Eventually, you'll be able to buy any of these items and you'll probably be able to get a better deal for yourself in the future.

2. Garage Sales:

Garage sales can be very easy to find and not a challenge for most. They can be a great opportunity to find good quality items at low prices. The best part is that there are usually no taxes.

You can find them in almost any residential area if you just drive around. People usually have them during the weekends, and when the weather is good.

Another good part about garage sales is that the seller is usually negotiable on the prices. They could be desperate and willing to let anything go for as much as half of the selling price. The best way to negotiate would be to strike up a friendly conversation. This can be really easy if you are a real people person. Simply say "I would love this item, but I cannot spend this much on it. Would you consider letting it go for "this lower amount". Make up an excuse if you have to, maybe there is a small scuff mark on the coffee table you're interested in and it would cost you money to repair it. It works a lot more than you'd think. Most of these people just want these items out of their house.

How to find a good garage sale:

Search through your local newspapers where you can find garage sale listings in the local classifieds.

Look through http://www.craigslist.org in your particular state and county to find garage sale listings.

Be on the lookout for fliers posted on telephone poles and bulletin boards at supermarkets.

Look out for Moving or Estate sales. These should be at the top of your list. These are sales that happen when the people cannot take the items with them.

If you happen to miss one of these and you're in the area anyway be sure to check the curb for any goods that may be put out for garbage for a free item. Remember that most people just want them out of their sight and out of their house!

Again, you Garage Sale of choice will depend on the amount of capital you have.

You have low capital:

Look for garage sales located in low-income residential areas. Here, you will find low-mid quality goods at a very low price. Most of the people having garage sales in these areas arestrapped for cash and will take anything you'll give them. Low ball offers accepted. Haggle away.

You have slightly higher capital:

Look for garage sales located in middle class areas. Here, you will find mid-high quality goods at a low price. The people in these areas are harder to haggle with. That should not stop you from trying. Even if you can get five dollars off of that awesome ride on lawnmower and you know someone will pay you another ten dollars over that amount, do it! Every little bit will add up, I promise!

You have very high capital:

There won't be many garage sales but you may be lucky! Your best bet is to search for estate sales in high end areas. Estate sales will help you find very high quality goods for a fraction of the price. This is where you'll find the good stuff! Search for those sought after items. Haggling may be difficult in these areas but let's hope you have enough experience at this point to know that almost anything is negotiable.

3. Flea Markets:

Flea markets are another place where you can find secondhand and brand new goods. A flea market is a place where the owner rents out "booths" or "stalls" where the vendor can set up shop and sell all sorts of items. Here, you will find various items at various prices. I will only recommend that you have a slightly higher to very high capital when purchasing these items.

You will find that flea markets get really busy with people looking for a good deal during any time of the year. There are rules you should follow when bargain hunting at a flea market. These people are trying to make money just like you are trying to.

Do not criticize the prices or products. These people make a living haggling. Everything here is negotiable. This is great for establishing relationships with vendors for future purchases. Be nice, courteous, and feel free to make friends here.

Do not let them hear you criticize a price or product out loud. It's disrespectful and they will not want to please a person who disrespects the way they make a living, so be friendly and respectful.

Here's a tip: Play the game. Ask to look at a product or ask for additional information about it. Such as where is it made or what the material it is made from. Seem interested and spend some time with the product. Then look or ask about the price. Use a facial expression that tells them that you will pass on the purchase. You'll find that the vendor will immediately drop the price to make a sale.

Trash = Treasure:

Another man's trash is another man's treasure. That's where you come in. Find a person who needs an item that you have and sell it to them. You will discover that you are not finding trash or junk. In the end you have become a treasure hunter.

Chapter 3: Finding Your Niche

You don't want to become overwhelmed in holding various products and not being able to sell them. You will need to find your niche. A niche is a particular type of items in a market. When you're confident with one niche, you may explore others. However, it's important to find one and stick with it at the beginning.

Start with the products that you know the most about. Perhaps you are a parent and you are experienced in buying baby and kid's clothes. Maybe you know a lot about electronics because you've been into them since you were a kid. If you are a musician, you may know a little or a lot about musical instruments. These are just examples. It is up to you to figure out what type of product will be the easiest for you to buy in confidence you are getting the best deal. In this chapter, we will go through the various items you will find in thrift stores and how they might relate to your particular niche.

Staying and continuing to sell in a niche will give you a reputation for being a great seller of that particular type of item. The best advertising is word of mouth. You will become more experienced in buying these particular items and increase your profits.

Remember to keep seasons and holidays in mind. Buy items that are out of season at a very low price and sell them right before the season starts for a good long-term profit. Try your hardest to sell on hand products as last minute holiday gifts.

Clothing and Shoes:

Everybody wears shoes and clothes. You already have experience in this if you wear clothes. What you may think is ugly or unfashionable could be beautiful and chic in someone else's eyes. It is best that you do become familiar with current trends, but it is not required when buying and selling these items.

Thrift Stores, Garage Sales, and Flea Markets are packed with secondhand clothing and shoes. When you look around these places, you will find that there is an almost unlimited supply of:

Baby Clothes and Shoes –

These are needed items for babies all year 'round and they are plentiful. Supply is high and demand is high. Buy as much as you can in various sizes, styles, and seasons. More than 300,000 babies are born in the US every year, and they need clothes. Moreover, growing babies go through a lot of cloths in different sizes. For this reason, consumers looking for a good deal do not want to spend an arm and a leg on an item that their babies will ruin or grow out of. Your profits will be low per item so you will need to sell a lot to see a good overall profit from these items.

Kids Clothes and Shoes –

Just like babies, kids go through clothes and shoes really fast. Buy a moderate amount of items that are in style. These items will cost a bit more than baby items but will still be cheap. Like babies, kids are constantly ruining clothes and shoes and they grow out of them fast! Profits should be moderate on each item sold.

Women's Clothes and Shoes –

Women generally know what they want, especially women who want a good deal. You're going to have to have a woman's mind or learn about the current styles to do well with these items. They will not be cheap, so hold out for those good deals. Shoes and boots are items that some women love. I would suggest buying a very moderate amount of shoes and clothing for women. Profits can be huge if you know what you're doing, but the sales will not be as easy.

Men's Clothes and Shoes –

The average male can be a very picky shopper for clothes. You're going to have to do some research on the latest trends to sell well with these items. They will not be extremely cheap, so hold out for those really good deals. A good tip, here, would be to learn the newest sneaker trends, sneaker heads can be impulse buyers. Try to stick to the items men might need such as boots, dress shoes, suits, and ties that are in good shape in various sizes. Buy a moderate amount of these. Profits can be huge but may be a harder sell.

A tip for long-term profits from shoes and clothing:

Buy those cute warm jackets in the summertime or summer clothes in the winter. They will be very cheap because they are out of season, especially when it comes to babies' or kids' items. Pack them away until the fall or spring for a long-term investment. They will sell fast and profitably.

Clothing Accessories -

You should purchase these items if you are going to sell clothing. Some accessories for clothing include: handbags, umbrellas, canes, ties, hats, belts, gloves, earmuffs, scarves, socks, stockings, etc... These items can be found in thrift stores, garage sales, and flea markets for cheap. You will find them in various sizes and styles.

Toys and Games:

We've all been children and some of you may have children. So we know that children are impulse buyers. They just don't want toys, they need them. As a result, parents also become impulse buyers when they are buying toys and games. You will find these items at almost all thrift stores, garage sales, and flea markets.

Some of the items you may find will probably be: board games, action figures, radio controlled vehicles, coloring books, dolls, stuffed animals, science toys, models, puzzles, play sets, cars, trucks, etc...The list is almost endless.

It is important that you inspect these items as most second hand toys run a high risk of being damaged, incomplete, or worn from children playing with them. Inspect that each item contains all pieces, is clean, and works correctly before purchasing. If the item takes batteries, check the compartment they should be in for evidence of corrosion. These items may be resealed inside of a box. Just ask permission from the seller for you to look and inspect the item before purchasing.

This is a great niche as long as you buy and sell good quality products. You can find these items relatively cheap and make great profits on them.

Electronics and Video Games:

This niche can be tricky if you do not know exactly what you're looking for. This is not a need in any sense, so when people are shopping for electronics and video games, they are searching for an item that they want.

In thrift stores, garage sales, and flea markets you may find: video game consoles, video games, alarm clocks, televisions, DVD/blue ray players, VCR players, stereo systems, cameras, video cameras, laptops/computers, portable audio players, phone, cell phones, and various other gadgets.

Be on the lookout for highly sought after items such as vintage video games, antique radios, and anything old that may be a collector's item that will bring you the big bucks.

It is important that you inspect these items and be sure they are not damaged and are in proper working order. There is a wide range of consumers looking for these products and it's a buyer's market. Meaning you would have to expect competition in this niche. If you buy the right items at the right prices, your profits can be great in this niche, but you need to have enough background information going in.

Appliances:

This niche is great if you have a good amount of capital. There is a want and a need for appliances in the US, where we have been accustomed to using them in our everyday lives. Keep in mind that you may need a large vehicle to transport and a place to store most of these items. The more you know about these items, especially if you can fix them, the easier they will be for you to sell.

In most thrift stores, garage sales, and flea markets, you may find: air conditioners, lamps, fans, electronic can openers, toasters, washers & dryers, dishwashers, stoves, electric griddles, irons, refrigerators, electronic space heaters, and much more!

It is very important that these items are safe. Be sure they are not damaged, and that they are in complete working order before you decide to sell them. If you hold out for really good prices on these items, the profits can be huge!

Furniture:

This niche can be very profitable. Keep in mind these items are mostly huge, so you will need a large vehicle for transporting furniture as well as a place to store them.

The more you know about these items, the easier they will be for you to buy and sell. The great thing about furniture is that they may be sold in sets at a lower price. Be on the lookout for vintage pieces that may be worth a lot of money!

Some of the furniture items you will find at thrift stores, garage sales, and flea markets include: tables, chairs, benches, couches, pool tables, cupboards, chests, wall units, beds, wardrobes, and much more. They will come in various styles and they'll be made of many materials such as wood, glass, and metals.

Most of these items will bear some type of damage from being used. It is important that you learn how to cover up scratches and be able to repair these items so you may resell them for a higher price than what you paid.

You may need a large amount of capital to buy these items and it may take time to sell them but your profits can be plentiful.

Pet Items:

Some see pet items as a necessity for their pets because they simply love them. This niche can be very profitable depending on how you market the products (we will get into that later in Chapter 4: Consumer Hunting).

Some of these items you'll be able to find at thrift stores, garage sales, and flea markets, but you will probably have a hard time finding a steady and good supply of them. The items that you should be looking for include: Cages, grooming supplies, harnesses & leashes, pet toys, feeders, beds, collars, tanks, and anything else that is pet related.

If these items are second hand, you want to make sure that they are clean and safe for pets. The people who are going to buy these items from you love their pets, so keep a good reputation and they may come back to buy more items.

You may need a moderate sized capital for this niche. As long as you can find a steady supply of goods at great prices you can do very well with pet items.

Everything Else:

Those were just a few good examples of the various types of items you can choose to buy and sell. When you walk into a thrift store, visit a garage sale, or take a trip to the flea market you'll find just about anything! Be on the lookout for items that people will want or need.

It's important that you find a niche because you need to build experience and a reputation in selling a particular type of item. The experience will help you market the item and sell it easily. Selling random items may wind up consuming every storage space you have available and eating away at your capital. Organization will be important in this part of the process. As your capital grows, you may move on to better and more profitable niches.

Chapter 4: Consumer Hunting

We are all consumers. If you bought this eBook, you are a consumer. Anyone who buys anything is a consumer. What does this tell us? Well for one, we are everywhere. This makes the hunt quite easy and simple.

In order to hunt for a consumer, you'll have to think like a consumer. Who are they buying an item for, what kind of item do they want, where can they buy this item, when can they receive this item, why should they buy this item, and how much will they spend?

In this chapter, we will discover the many hunting grounds where you will find your consumers. The chase can be frustrating and tedious, but you must be willing to put yourself out there to make the sale.

There are many free and inexpensive ways to promote the sale of your items. You can sell items right from home easily. You may also meet potential buyers in a public place such as a parking lot in front of a local convenience store. You may also arrange to send an item to a seller's address.

There are some precautions you should keep in mind. Be sure to use the proper precautions when meeting a seller face to face. Always make sure, in advance, the seller will have the correct amount of money if paying in cash so you won't need to bring change. Only meet in a brightly lit public area. Bring a friend or family member to help you complete a transaction if you are unsure. It is better to be safe than sorry.

Promote your item physically:

List your items in local classifieds in the local newspapers or Penny saver advertisement papers. This may cost you some money, but it is an effective way to sell items that people need, especially at the beginning before you establish a customer base.

Post flyers around town. I'm sure you've seen flyers posted before. Use the telephone poles, supermarket bulletin boards, or anywhere that you are allowed to legally post a flyer.

Promote your item virtually:

Use http://www.craigslist.org to post your item online for the people who are searching for good deals on items in your area.Use the wanted section to give you a good idea on the types of items that are in demand.

Use http://www.ebay.com to auction or sell your item globally. This is the largest marketplace for used items, and it is very well-known. Take note that there are selling and shipping fees that are applied to items listed on this site, and that you must use a registered and approved account to list an item on eBay.

Use http://www.amazon.com to sell your item globally. This is a great place to sell used items. Take note that there are selling and shipping fees that are applied to items listed on this site, and that you must use a registered and approved account to list on Amazon.

Use http://www.facebook.com to sell your item locally. Yes, that's right; Facebook can help you sell your items. If you are unfamiliar with this concept, we will explain it to you. If you have a Facebook account, there will be groups you can join to sell your item. At the top of the page type in "sell" and hit the search button. Then click "groups" under the "more" tab. You will find local groups that have thousands of members that will see your ad when you post it. Click "add" next to as many groups as you want and wait for your approval before posting. It's very easy and simple to use. You may even find people asking for items, so be sure to pay attention to them. Best of all, it's absolutely free! Be sure to read and abide by all the rules of every group.

These are the best ways to promote your item and get thousands of eyes on your stock. You may use any of these items in conjunction with each other and cancel all other listings after you have found your buyer. Be sure to read all the rules and realize that there may be a fee for pulling an item from sites such as eBay. You should also be aware that sales sometimes fall through. It happens. Just relist and keep moving on.

Once you have made contact with a buyer, be sure to be nice and courteous; be the best seller you can possibly be. You should know a great amount about your niche by now, so start up a conversation about the piece that is being sold and suggest a similar item that you have on hand to make another sale right away. The worst that can happen is for the buyer to say no.

If the buyers seem pleased with the service you offered, let them know that you will be getting more items very soon and to ask them to let anyone else who might be looking for a similar item to come to you.

Chapter 5: Effectively Describing Items

So you know what you're selling, where to buy your items, who to sell them to, and where to list them. Do you know how to effectively describe and sell your item? In this chapter, we will show you how to effectively describe your item.

Get rid of the guesswork for the buyer right off the bat. In order to effectively describe your item, you must provide a brief and detailed description of the item you are trying to sell. The more detailed your description is, the better luck you will have selling it.

State exactly what the item is that you're selling. You may want to do some research on the general aspects of the product. State the name, model, and manufacturer of the product as the title. In the brief description, list the details such as:

- Year it was made.
- Materials it is made from.
- The condition it is in.
- Size/Dimensions.

- Color of the item.
- If the item is used or not.

Avoid selling products that may be illegal in your state/county. Even though you may have bought it legally, it doesn't mean you can sell it legally. If you are unsure, then you should check with local laws.

Don't use any information in the description of your item that isn't true. Try to be as brief as possible without leaving any details out of the description.

Chapter 6: Growing Profits to a Steady Income

After learning how to buy items, how to market them and how to sell them to potential clients, you hopefully started making a good profit. This is not the end of the road, however. Hold on for one more moment before you spend a single penny. If you spend your profit now, you'll have to start the whole process over to get it back. You need a way to reach your goal of $3000+ per month.

You must have a strong willpower to not spend a single cent until your profits reach your goal each month. You must let it ride in order to grow your profits.

The reason behind this is simple. You're going to take your initial capital we'll call that (C). Then, we will take your profit and call that (P). Once your profit (P) minus your initial capital (C) equals your goal (G) you will have reached the financial freedom you've worked so hard for.

C – P = G

Example:

Let's say you start out with $50, an easily obtainable capital. If you can double that by your first month you will have $100. At the start of your second month you will have $100 (C+P) to buy used goods. If you can double that, you'll have $200 to invest in the third month. By the end of month three you should have $400. If you add your capital to your profit each month by the end of the 6th month you will have made $3200. If you continue after that you may start spending your profit.

C x 2 = P will be the result at the end of each month.

Month 1 = $100, Month 2 = $200, Month 3 = $400

Month 4 = $800 Month 5 = $1600 Month 6 = $3200

By month 6, you will have made $3150 profit. $3200 (C-P). As long as you keep using all of the money you made from month 6 you'll hold the same profits each month after. At 7 months, you will continue to pull in 3000+ each month. The more money you start with the faster you will achieve your goals. Good Luck!

Conclusion

Thank you again for downloading this book!

I hope this book was able to help you to earn $3000+ each month.

The next step is to get out there and start making money!

Finally, if you enjoyed this book, please take the time to share your thoughts and post a review on Amazon. It'd be greatly appreciated!

Thank you and good luck!

Book # 2

Garage Sales

The Ultimate Beginner's Guide to Making Killer Profits from Garage Sales in 30 Minutes or Less!

Copyright © 2015

All rights reserved. No part of this book may be reproduced in any form without permission in writing from the author. Reviewers may quote brief passages in reviews.

Disclaimer

No part of this publication may be reproduced or transmitted in any form or by any means, mechanical or electronic, including photocopying or recording, or by any information storage and retrieval system, or transmitted by email without permission in writing from the publisher.

While all attempts and efforts have been made to verify the information held within this publication, neither the author nor the publisher assumes any responsibility for errors, omissions, or opposing interpretations of the content herein.

This book is for entertainment purposes only. The views expressed are those of the author alone, and should not be taken as expert instruction or commands. The reader of this book is responsible for his or her own actions when it comes to reading the book.

Adherence to all applicable laws and regulations, including international, federal, state, and local governing professional licensing, business practices, advertising, and all other aspects of doing business in the US, Canada, or any other jurisdiction is the sole responsibility of the purchaser or reader.

Neither the author nor the publisher assumes any responsibility or liability whatsoever on the behalf of the purchaser or reader of these materials.

Any received slight of any individual or organization is purely unintentional.

Contents

Introduction

Chapter 1: Garage Sale Basics

Chapter 2: When to organize a garage sale

Chapter 3: How to Properly Price Your Items

Chapter 3: Garage Sale Ads

Chapter 4: Rules and Tips For Successful Garage Sale

Chapter 5: Why are Garage Sales Profitable for Buyers Too

Chapter 6: Garage Sale Fun Facts

Conclusion

Introduction

First and foremost, I want to thank you for downloading the book, "Garage Sales – The Ultimate Beginner's Guide to Making Killer Profits from Garage Sales in 30 Minutes or Less!".

In this book you will learn how to plan your own garage sale. Also, you will learn all the steps you will need to take before you display the items you are selling for people to purchase. Garage sales are the only way of getting rid of the stuff you don't want or need anymore, it is great a way of earning money, connecting with people and teaching your children some responsibility.

This Garage sale basics book will teach you more about the concept of holding a garage sale, in addition all the reasons why people decide to have one. Additionally, this book will teach you when is the right time of year, the day, and time to organize your garage sale in order to gain more profits.

You don't have to worry about how you are going to price your items, because this book contains a special section where you will learn how to set a price for certain items, baby clothes, adult clothing, furniture, antiques, decorative items, electronics and kitchen appliances. Further, you will learn more about how to properly price your items and how to track your sales correctly.

Garage sales simply can't be successful without flyers and advertisements, therefore this book will teach you how to write the perfect ad and flyer that will attract more visitors, and what to include, and what not to include.

Basic garage sale tips, advice and tricks are included here so you will know how to conduct your garage sale and how to treat the people who attend.

To make things more interesting, this book contains fun facts about the history of garage sales.

Thanks again for downloading this book, I hope you enjoy it!

Chapter 1: Garage Sale Basics

Garage sales have been part of our culture and tradition for hundreds of years, however most people miss all of the fun in being a part of garage sales (buyers + sellers). There is more to it then to just buying and selling items. Garage sales are opportunities to bring people together while still making money or finding that special item you have always wanted.

The purpose of this book is to explain the concept of garage sales and to teach you how to make a big profits for yourself.

What is a Garage Sale

Garage sales are informal events where people sell their used goods. Sellers at garage sales are not required to have a business license or need to collect sales tax.

Garage sales are also known by the terms, yard sale, junk sale, attic sale, or basement sale.

Items that can be found at garage sales include books, toys, clothes, furniture, sports equipment, kitchen appliances etc. Basically, everything someone no longer needs can be included in their garage sale.

Why to Hold a Garage Sale

Garage sales can be organized for several reasons and they include:

- Eliminating things a person no longer wants or need anymore – garage sales are perfect events for people to finally get rid of clothing and furniture that you no longer need. Also, if your children have grown up, there really is no need to keep their baby clothes, or toys. So instead of keeping them in your attic or basement, you can actually profit from selling these items.

- Make someone happy – believe it or not, there are people who love buying used stuff at garage sales. These people are bargain and treasure hunters, and they like old stuff, and sometimes garage sales offer things they are unable to find at the store. Organizing a garage sale is the perfect way to make someone happy and earn you some money along the way.

- Earn money – well, who says garage sales can't make you more money? Sure they can. Instead of just letting that old stuff get in your way and cluttering up your house, you can be smart, and sell them. With a smart organization technique, right pricing, and a well-written garage sale ad, you can earn more than you can imagine.

- Make space for things you care about – selling stuff you don't need is a perfect way to make room in your home for the things you do love. First, your house, including the attic and basement will be clutter-free, basically anywhere you are storing things you don't need. Second, you get to conduct a little makeover of your house. You will make room for the new things you want, because you will now have all the free space you need.

- Meeting new people – garage sales are perfect occasions to meet your neighbors, and new people. Additionally, you will meet bargain hunters who will inform you about other garage sales where you might find something you would like. If you're new in the neighborhood, this is a perfect opportunity to meet your neighbors, and get to know them better.

- Fund-raising – people often throw a garage sale to raise money for a certain causes. It is a win-win situation – you get rid of the stuff you don't want or need anymore, and along the way you are able to help someone.

- Purchasing other stuff – unfortunatly you can't earn millions of dollars, but the money you do gain from your garage sales can and will help you purchase something else you want, but possibly didn't have enough funds to get before.

- Teaching kids about business and responsibility – garage sales are ideal for parents who want to teach their children how to conduct a business, and how to be responsible with their money. It's a perfect way to show them the value of a dollar, and how hard work, and being wise pays off. Not only that, you are also teaching them to respect other people (customers), and to respect other stuff around the house (as you might need them to help you organize your next garage sale).

Chapter 2: When to organize a garage sale

If you want your garage sale to be successful and to make a significant amount of money, then it is important to pick the best date and time for the event.

Naturally, garage sales require careful organization. You cannot just decide to throw the event, take your stuff out and hope for the best. Your goal is making money, and it won't come without the right schedule, careful consideration, and thorough planning.

Throughout this chapter, we will talk about organizing the garage sale and picking the right month, date, and time of your event.

Let's face it, everything revolves around careful planning and having the right organization. If you want to make a killer profit by selling things you don't use anymore, then you need a detailed plan about what time of the year is the best for your garage sale, what day of the week will get the most profit, and when should your garage sale open and close.

Your entire profit doesn't only depend on the things that people buy, but it also depends on the right timing.

Timing is the factor that can either make, or break your garage sale and its profit.

If you are a first-time seller, pay close attention to our advice for choosing the best time to hold your garage sale.

Best Month

Considering you will need to move all of your stuff outside, and stay outside until your garage sale is over, the best time of the year for a garage sale is during spring.

Spring is ideal because unlike winter there aren't cold temperatures, and snow.

Early spring garage sales are the most popular, it is also the time when you are able to earn more money.

If you're not a fan of spring, or simply can't organize everything at that time, then your next best opportunity is the second Saturday in August. It is also known as National Garage Sale Day. Summer garage sales are also popular, and throwing one on the National Garage sale day can guarantee the most money.

FUN FACT: National Garage Sale Day is an idea started in 2001 by C. Daniel Rhodes from Alabama. He noticed his neighbors had garage sales on different weekends, and realized everyone would make more profit if garage sales were held on the same day.

Garage sales thrown at the end of summer can be as successful as those in early spring. So, if you want to throw a garage sale, make sure you pick early spring or late summer. Additonally, when you choose the month, it is always best to have garage sale at the beginning of that month. It will make more money than garage sales held at the end of the month.

Best Day

When you decide the time of the year and the month of your garage sale, it is important to choose what time it will be. Naturally, week days are not a good idea because people work during the week, they are also busy and simply don't have time to visit various garage sales. And let's face it, you might have a job too, or you have to pick up your kids from school, so week days are not also good for you.

The best days for garage sales are Friday, Saturday, and Sunday.

Friday – is good if your home is located near any busy roads during lunch or after work.

Saturday – is always the best day to throw a garage sale. Most people have their best sales on Saturdays. They have enough time to organize everything, people whom come are generally off of work and have the time to visit different garage sales.

Sunday – are not as profitable as Saturdays. But there is significant traffic, and Sundays are usually the day when people are on the hunt to find a specific item. There are people who visit garage sales every Sunday to look for items that can't be bought anywhere else.

The Bottom line is, if you want your garage sale to be successful, try to organize it on Saturday as that is the most profitable day for your event.

Garage sales on Friday and Sunday should be organized when:

- You have a specific or hard-to-find item that you want to sell
- If Friday or Sunday is an "open house" day in your neighborhood, (it's usually Sunday)

- If your garage sale is multi-day sale.

Best Time

If you want your garage sale to be successful (and you do), then you can't obviously start at noon. Even though garage sales are held during weekends, one might think there is no need to hurry as people choose that time to sleep in. That is wrong.

The busiest time for the garage sale is between 7AM and 11AM. Also, that period of time can determine the success of your sale for the remainder of the day.

People who visit garage sales get up early and are are ready to go. Hence, the earlier you start, the more successful it will be. People often find they begin taking items out of their homes to sale only to find a group of cars already waiting.

In order to be ready before your customers arrive and have more success, make sure your garage sale is organized and ready to start at 7AM.

REMEMBER: it is important to be organized and prepare everything early. Otherwise, you will always be step behind. Your goal is to make a killer profit with your garage sale, and that includes the proper organization.

The closing time of your garage sale should be between 1PM and 3PM.

Additional Tips for Choosing the Time and Date for Garage Sale

- April and August are the best months for holding garage sales
- Coordinate the time and date with other garage sales in your neighborhood
- Organizing a community sale in the early spring, or late summer can double or triple the number of the visitors, which also means more profit.
- When organizing, you should also check the weather forecast for that day. You don't want your garage sale ruined by poor weather.

Chapter 3: How to Properly Price Your Items

Pricing items that you want to include in your garage sale can oftentimes be challenging if you don't remember how much you paid for it originally.

Keep in mind that people who visit garage sales are there because they are hunting for bargains. They don't, and won't pay more money for something, so don't overprice items.

Pricing is an important part of your garage sale success and profit. Most people are always uncertain how to price items and think they should place a higher price on certain items. One thing is for certain, it will be easier for you after your first garage sale. You will know what items sold better, and what prices were acceptable to people.

And who said you can't make a significant profit on your first garage sale? In order to make a big profit with your very first garage sale, follow our tips about pricing.

Pricing Tips

- Baby clothes should be priced between $1 and $3. Don't price them higher, unless they are branded with the tag still attached. If they tag is still attached, we recommend pricing it up to $5.

- If the baby clothes are stained, or not in good shape then you should price them between $0.25 and $0.50 (because you just want to get rid of them anyway, plus nobody's going pay more for damaged or stained clothing).

- If you have a lot of baby clothes and you aren't sure if you will need them anymore, then you should make a special offer. For example, three baby shirts for $4 dollars, or an entire bag of baby clothes for between $5 and $10.

- Adult clothing should be priced at between $3 and $5. Make sure you don't price your old clothes higher than this, because shoppers can find them cheaper at someone else's garage sale. Plus, your goal is to make a profit and get rid of the stuff anyway. If the clothing is made by a famous brand, and still has a tag on it, then you can price it a little higher.

- Your shoes should be priced between $5 and $7.

- Price your coats between $10 and $15.

- When it comes to books, price them at $1, if the cover is beautifully designed or if the book is a rare edition, consider asking for more money. Remember, don't overprice. Your item shouldn't be as expensive or cost the same as the items sold in stores.

- If you have a lot of DVDs you want to sell, price them at $5, and CDs should be priced at $3.

- In order to sell as much as you can and get more profit, you should arrange special offers for these items also. For example, three books for $2.50, three DVDs for $10, and so on. You can even mix them up, e.g. two DVDs and one CD for $10. Be creative. Your goal is to sell as much as possible, so you have the freedom to design all kinds of special offers.

- Board games should be priced between $5 and $10.

- If you are selling old furniture that you don't need that is cluttering up your basement or attic then you should price them correctly in order to sell faster. Price furniture of low quality between $10 and $30.

- Furniture of higher quality should be priced between $50 and $75. The rule for pricing higher quality furniture for garage sales is: you should charge 1/3 of the original price. If you paid your nightstand or table $300, then you can even ask for $100 for it at your garage sale. However, if you are going to ask for 1/3 of the original price, make sure the furniture is in great condition.

- Rare antiques should be priced at $100 and more – if you have something valuable, but still want to sell it because you either don't use it anymore, don't need it, or don't have place for it, then you should start with $100. Bear in mind that you have to check the value of those items on the market. Go online and see how much items like that cost and decide on the price according to your research. Additionally, before you brand something as a rare antique, make sure it really is.

- Decorative items should be priced between $3 and $5. Items like mirrors, candlesticks, and pictures should belong in the lower-priced items at your garage sale (unless they are antiques).

- Computer equipment and some appliances should be priced at $20 or lower. Don't pay attention to how much you paid for these items, because asking for more will result in your customer leaving to find a better offer. Appliances like juicers, or toasters aren't expensive to begin with, so they can't be priced higher. Computer equipment is always changing, technology advances, so you really can't ask for more for the old equipment you don't even use anymore.
- Kitchen supplies like plates, spoons, forks etc. should be priced at between $1 and $3.

Toys should be priced between $1 and $3. Also, if you have a lot of toys, you can make special offers for them too.

Additional Pricing Tips

Along with proper pricing, you have to pay attention to the tags you place on your items, and other price-related tasks. Additional pricing tips include:

- Have your own tagging system, especially if you ask your friends and family to help you. Every person should have different colored tags.

- Even though some sellers use them, you SHOULD NOT use color-coded dot stickers. The purpose of this is to attach certain colored dot to the items, and then place the pricin chart nearby. The truth is, buyers find this system frustrating, so avoid doing it.

- Prices should be displayed large and clear.

- If you are selling paper-made items, don't use sticker tags or tape.

Don't write the price directly on the merchandice. Use tags. They are available everywhere, and are fairly inexpeinsive. The price should be on top of the merchandice, not at the bottom.

- When pricing furniture, you should use bigger tag or piece of paper to make it clear and visible.

- If there is a significant event, or special bit of information about a piece of antique furniture, or old items you want to sell, point it out, e.g. "coffee table, has been in our family since 1961"

- Point out relevant information about appliances, for example, if vacuum cleaner is corded, cordless and make sure to include what type of battery it needs if it takes batteries.

- Offer an item for free with every purchase. There are a lot of items, like toys, or if you can't sell absolutely every DVD from your collection. Buyers appreciate gifts, and make sure to point out that every buyer gets a certain item for free with their purchase. This will increase traffic and result in a good profit.

- Don't mention how you can sell the item for higher price on eBay. Let's face it, if you could, then you would have done it. And also, it's not a nice way of handling buyers at garage sales.

- Make sure items are priced the same way you'd want them to be if you decided to visit someone else's garage sale. Think this:"Would I want to buy this for this price?", if the answer is "No.", then change the price.

Chapter 3: Garage Sale Ads

If you want to make killer profits from your garage sale you need a lot of traffic. You are aware that traffic depends on the number of people that visit your garage sale, and eventually make a purchase.

People who don't live in your neighborhood and those who don't have any kind of relationship with you, can't magically know you're throwing garage sale on a certain date.

When you decide to organize your garage sale, make sure you post a lot of garage sale ads, and flyers that will inform people about the sale, location, date and time.

In this chapter, you will learn how to make your own garage sale ad that will attract a lot of people and what to put in these ads. Additionally, you will learn how to make your garage sale ad stand out and get more attention.

Good Garage Sale Ad Needs

In order to create the good garage sale ad, you have to know what the ad should include. Garage sale ads can be published online. When creating a garage sale ad you should:

- Along with online ads, consider publishing it in the local newspapers, to get more visitors
- You need to create a title that will automatically get more attention
- Create similar text for ads and flyers
- Instead of just listing the items you want to send, describe them in one sentence.
- When naming clothes, mention sizes, brands, and other information.
- Tell potential buyers why they should visit your garage sale
- Be honest about the items' condition. Don't make this information up, and don't sugar-coat anything. People understand that items at garage sales are used and not in perfect condition, so just be honest.
- Try to include a couple of photos

- If you live in a widely-populated area, include a photo of a landmark near you, so the people can find you easily

- If you don't want your garage sale to start in the morning (and you should), then make sure your ad has the right time written on it

- Don't use cliché "Everything must go". It's a garage sale after all. It is obvious you are trying to sell everything, this just wastes space on your ad. Your mission is to make your ad stand out, you don't want to make it similar to someone else's.

- Even though you need to include the time when your garage sale starts, you are not obligated to include the closing time. Sometimes, the closing time just lets people know how desperate you are to sell you items, so they can use that fact as leverage against you in an effort to get a better deal.

- If you do include the closing time, be prepared for the last-minute bargain shoppers and competiton between buyers (in case they both want the same thing). If you don't have many items to sell, then a closing time might not be a bad idea, instead point out, it is a "limited time offer".

- To make your ad stand out, don't forget to mention any collectible or rare items you want to sell. This will attract more buyers.

- Your ads should be published at least one week before your garage sale. When it comes to online ads, you can choose to place it on local free websites like Craigslist.com, or Backpage.com. The day before your garage sale, don't forget to post a reminder.

- The same ad that is published on Craigslist.com, or in newspapers can be published on your social media profiles like Facebook, or Google+. This will attract even more potential buyers to your garage sale.

- If you are creating a community garage sale, with your neighbors, then include your ad in the local newspapers events section.

- NOTE: if you are organizing a multi-day garage sale, then treat it seperately, i.e. publish separate ads for each day. Why? Because if people see a multi-day ad they will assume if they arrive on the second day of your garage sale that all good stuff will be gone. Treating every day separately will bring in a bigger profit.

- When including photos in your ad on Craigslist.com, do NOT upload them directly to the website, because their clarity will decrease. Instead, choose some photohosting website like Flickr.com, or Photobucket.com and include the link to your Cragislist ad.

Tips for People in Rural Areas

If you live in a rural area, and you can't rely on traffic or a lot of people seeing your ad. In order to have successful garage sale, you should:

- Publish the ad one or two weeks before the garage sale
- Make sure you place your ads in nearby towns
- Advertise in newspapers
- Coordinate the date of your garage sale with a big event that takes place in your town.
- Place street signs in places with more traffic

- Include detailed instructions about the location

- Involve neighbors or family to get more visitors.

REMEMBER: if, for any reason, you change your mind or something happens and you're not able to have your garage sale, make sure you cancel the ads, or to use your social media accounts etc. to let everybody know there won't be garage sale. That is the responsible thing to do.

Garage Sale Flyers

The flyers that inform people about your garage sale should include:

- Listed items that will be included in the garage sale

- Photos

- Details about date, location, and time

- Tell people why they should visit your garage sale

- And also, never use "Everything must go"

Headlines That Will Attract More Attention

Naturally, the attention of readers and passers-by need to be grabbed with the headline. Some of the headlines that are good for garage sales include:

- HUGE RANGE OF ITEMS
- BIG CLEAN OUT
- BARGAIN HUNTER'S GARAGE SALE
- 10% OF SALES TO BE DONATE TO CHARITY (and make sure you do that)
- ANNUAL GARAGE SALE
- STUFF TO RESELL
- PERFECT STUFF FOR EBAY, BUT I AM TOO LAZY
- IF I WERE YOU, I WOULD BUY SOMETHING
- ONE DAY GARAGE SALE AT_____, ON_____

Additional Info

When publishing flyers, you should:

- Browse Google images to get some ideas

- Include tear-offs (little slips they can tear off the paper with the garage sale information)

- Place them on community boards and in shop windows

- Send flyers to second-hand shop owners

- Make your own signs (be creative)

- If you don't like doing arts and crafts, you can buy signs on sassysigns.com, and websites like Amazon, and Garage Sale Tools.

To sum it up, you can publish your ads on social media outlest, Craigslist, and local newspapers. Also, you can make all sorts of flyers to inform people about your garage sale. Be specific, include a lot of details, and don't use too many cliches.

Chapter 4: Rules and Tips For Successful Garage Sale

Garage sales aren't easy and require a lot of time. It is especially tough on people who are throwing their first garage sale. In order to make things easier, and to simplify the entire process, below are tips and rules to make your first garage sale profitable and successful.

Tips and Rules for profitable Garage Sale

- Collect enough stuff – before you decide to throw a garage sale, make sure you have enough stuff that you want to sell. This may sound too simple, but people often find it hard to get rid of something, or sell it, even though they have already decided they will include that specific item in their sale.

- Ask someone to help you – you will not be able to do it all by yourself. Garage sales require a lot of work, so asking your spouse, friends, or family to help is a good idea. Also, on the day of the sale you can ask your teenager to help.

- Move your car – your car should not be parked in front of your house. You should leave this parking space open to the potential buyer

- Sale items don't have to be from inside your house – you can include gardening tools, or plants in your garage sale.

- As already mentioned, give something for free in order to gain more profit.

- Visit different garage sales before throwing your own. See how they price and display items and conduct their sale.

- Make sure all merchandise you want to sell is nicely displayed. Don't just throw it out on your lawn and leave it there.

- Remember how to price your items – the prices shouldn't be too high, nor too low. And ask yourself if you would pay that much for the item.

- Make lemonade or ice tea and offer it to buyers.

- Be friendly, but also remain in the background – when a buyer arrives, say hello and be friendly. However, nobody likes a pushy seller, don't follow your customers around. Give them their own space to shope and time to think about whether they want something or don't.

- When choosing items for sale, make sure you include as much items as possible. You never know what someone is looking for, so offer a wide variety of products.

- The most interesting items should be closer to the curb to get a buyers' attention.

- You need to make sure you have enough change in the form of small bills and coins.

- Keep money in a safe place

- If the product you want to sell comes with the original box, keep it, and offer it to your buyer.

- Before the garage sale, come up with a plan of what are you going to do with the unsold products. You can decide to save them for another garage sale, or you can donate them.

- Before the garage sale, check to see if your city or town has a law that requires getting a permit for a garage sale. If so, get one.

- Arrange the tables, and place all merchandise carefully.

- Clothes should be on a hanger, or folded nicely.

- Make sure everything you sell (clothes, shoes, toys, furniture etc.) are clean. Nobody likes to buy dirty stuff.

- At least one hour before the garage sale starts, you should be outside, sorting everything, arranging signs etc.

- If you are throwing your garage sale during summer, bring a fan to make your buyers more comfortable in the heat.

- If you have helpers, make sure the person who's handling the money is good with the math (if you don't have time to do it yourself)

- Count the change back to your customer, and make sure they see how much money you are giving to them.

- Make sure you have a SOLD sign on furniture etc. that a person can't take home right away.

- Make sure you have a tape measure in case someone wants to purchase something but are not sure about the dimensions.

Safety Tips

While garage sales are practical, they attract a lot of people (even people you don't know), so you have to be careful and remember these tips:

- Never talk about how much money you are making
- Never let anyone in your house
- Lock all your doors
- Every helper you have needs to know what their role is.
- Don't ignore your customers, don't chit chat and ignore what your customers are doing
- If you have pets, keep them inside.
- When it comes to negotiating and bargain, don't do it right away. Start around noon, (you don't want to give everything away for less money than you wanted too early).

Preparing for Garage Sale

Your garage sale items need to be prepared, but you have to be ready also. Here are some ideas.

- Get enough sleep the night before

- Come up with a to-do list where you keep everything you need to do in the morning. The list will remind you in the event you forget to do something. Keeping a list is key for good organization and planning.

- Make sure everything is priced, unpacked, and ready

- Open your garage door according to the schedule

- Rearrange items from time to time to make tables look full after other merchandise has sold.

- When the sale is over, clean everything, remove all the signs, and pack everything carefully.

Garage sales require a lot of work, however with the help you can do it easily. Make sure everything is priced the right way, be polite, and include helpers with different tasks.

Your first garage sale can be profitable if you follow and pay attention to all the advice and tips we have offered in this book.

NOTE: If the closing time (or if it's afternoon and there is relatively not much traffic), and you still have a lot of stuff left – don't despair.

Just go around with your price tags, and lower their price. You can also come up with a new offer for the next buyer to ensure they will make a purchase. Everything can be done with a little bit of creativity, and your garage sale can be profitable and successful, but also it is great lesson for your next garage sale.

Chapter 5: Why are Garage Sales Profitable for Buyers Too

Garage sales aren't only good for sellers. They are good for buyers too. It can be said that garage sales are a win-win situation, where both sides close the deal happy and satisfied.

People visit garage sales for numerous reasons like:

- They like good deals
- They like to bargain
- They like socializing with other people from different neighborhoods
- People visit garage sales because they can find hidden treasures
- Garage sales are good sources of quality things for a lower price
- They need things for a collection
- They love to buy broken things and fix them
- They love to buy and sell various things to sell on eBay

- Some people actually buy stuff at garage sales and sell them for a living.

Most Popular Garage Sale Items

As it was already mentioned, garage sales are win-win situations. Here is a list of most-searched for items, and most popular items at garage sales to make even more profit:

- Old cellphones – teenagers love to buy them, and resell them on eBay.
- Baby clothes, shoes, and toys
- Magazines, or comic books – appreciated by collectors
- Wedding-related items
- Pregnancy clothes
- Power tools (saws, drills, etc.)
- Sports equipment
- Electronics
- Bicycles

- Household appliances (refrigerator, irons, dicers, juicers)

- Books

- Furniture

- Gardening equipment

- Jewelry (rings, watches, necklaces)

- Beddings

- Shoes, boots, and coats

- Linens, especially vintage.

Famous Garage Sale Purchases

- In the year 2000, Rick Norsigian purchased some glass plates for $45 at the Los Angeles warehouse salvage sale. Later, it was confirmed that the glass plates were actually original photographic negatives by the famous nature photographer Ansel Adams. The real worth of these negatives today is $200,000,000.

- In the year 2008, Tony Marohn bought a box which contained old papers at a garage sale for $5 and later discovered they were certificates for an oil company that was acquired by Coca Cola. Today they are worth – 130,000,000.

- In the year 2012, a man bought an art sketch for only $5. It was discovered later that sketch was actually Andy Warhol's original painting worth $2,000,000.

Ideally, you have lots of items that fit into more categories, and with the right ads, flyers, and pricing, you can make a significant profit.

If you offer nice services and reasonable prices, you can even ask buyers to leave their phone number so you can contact them when you decide to arrange your next garage sale. They will recommend you to others, and your items so the next event can be even more profitable.

Also, bear in mind that you need buyers as much as they need you. Without your buyers you wouldn't be able to get rid of all your stuff and to make a lot of profit (that is your goal after all). That is why you have to be patient, and polite.

Chapter 6: Garage Sale Fun Facts

In order to make garage sales even more interesting than they are, here are some fun facts that will inspire you to throw your own garage sale event.

- In the early 1800s, garage sales were different. Unclaimed cargo was sold in shipping yards at discounted price. The events were called "rommage sales".

- In the late 1800s rommage sales became rummage sales, and their location moved from the shipping docs to charity bazaars, or churches and other community spaces.

- Garage sales as we know them today, started in the 1950s or 1960s after World War II. As cities were expanding and people were looking for houses with garages and yards increased.

- Through the 1970s and 1990s garage sales become even more popular as the economy grew, people are constantly in demand for new products and merchandise. As a result, they want to sell or get rid of products they have owned before.

- In the 1990s and 2000's, people used the internet in order to find all the garage sales in their area. That is when garage sale ads become popular online, and in newspapers too.

- Now, there are even apps where people are able to find all garage sales in their area. Not only that, people are even able to find out what items they can find at certain locations. With the rise of internet, the popularity of good deals garage sales grew (that is why your ads have to be perfect which will guarantee the profit).

- The world's longest garage sale is The 127 Corridor Sale – held on National Garage Sale Day (already mentioned above; the second Saturday in August) and it spans 690 miles along Highway 127 from Michigan all the way to Alabama. Thousands of sellers participated in this event.

Garage Sale in Numbers

165,000 – the estimated number of garage sales every week in the United Sates.

690,000 – the estimated number of buyers who purchased something at garage sales every week.

4,967,500 – the estimated number of items and products that are sold at garage sales every week.

$4,222,375 – the estimated total US weekly revenue from garage sales.

$0.85 – the estimated average price of garage sale item.

Conclusion

Thank you again for downloading this book!

I hope this book helped you to learn more about garage sales, its purposes, rules and pricings. The goal of this book was to help you create and run your very own garage sale and earn killer profits.

The next step upon successful completion of this book is to start deciding what items should be at your garage sale, decide when to throw your event, and check if you need to acquire any permits. If not, go ahead and get rid of that old stuff that you don't use anymore and earn some money.

Throughout this book you now understand that garage sales require a lot of patience and dedication. Also, not only are they are helpful, they are one of the activities that has been a part of our culture for hundreds of years.

Now that you know how to plan, conduct, and price the items that will be included in your garage sale.

Go ahead, start your own garage sale and make some money.

Finally, if you enjoyed this book, please take the time to share your thoughts and post a review on Amazon. It'd be greatly appreciated!

Thank you and good luck!

www.ingramcontent.com/pod-product-compliance
Lightning Source LLC
Chambersburg PA
CBHW021003180526
45163CB00005B/1875